ADULT COLORING BOOK

Baby Animals

This book belongs to

_____

_____

A Guide to Using This Book

There are a total of 50 unique drawings in this book.

Be sure to use soft-colored sharp pencils to get better results.

Be careful of using other tools such as gel pens or markers. We recommend a piece of cardstock or thick paper behind the page you're working on to prevent the ink from bleeding to the page below.

Use a color test page to try out different colors to find the best combinations as you expect. Be cautious; colors might vary from your expectations sometimes.

Color whichever images you feel like at the moment and skip whichever you want to. You can come back the next day as we advised you to practice daily to get the most out of this experience.

Share Your Creativity. Why keep that creativity hidden? Why keep that creativity hidden? We encourage you to share your colored pages with like-minded colorists just like you. We would love to see your art masterpiece.

It doesn't end here. Visit our website to unlock the hidden page and join our Facebook Group Damita Victoria Artwork to get more free images.

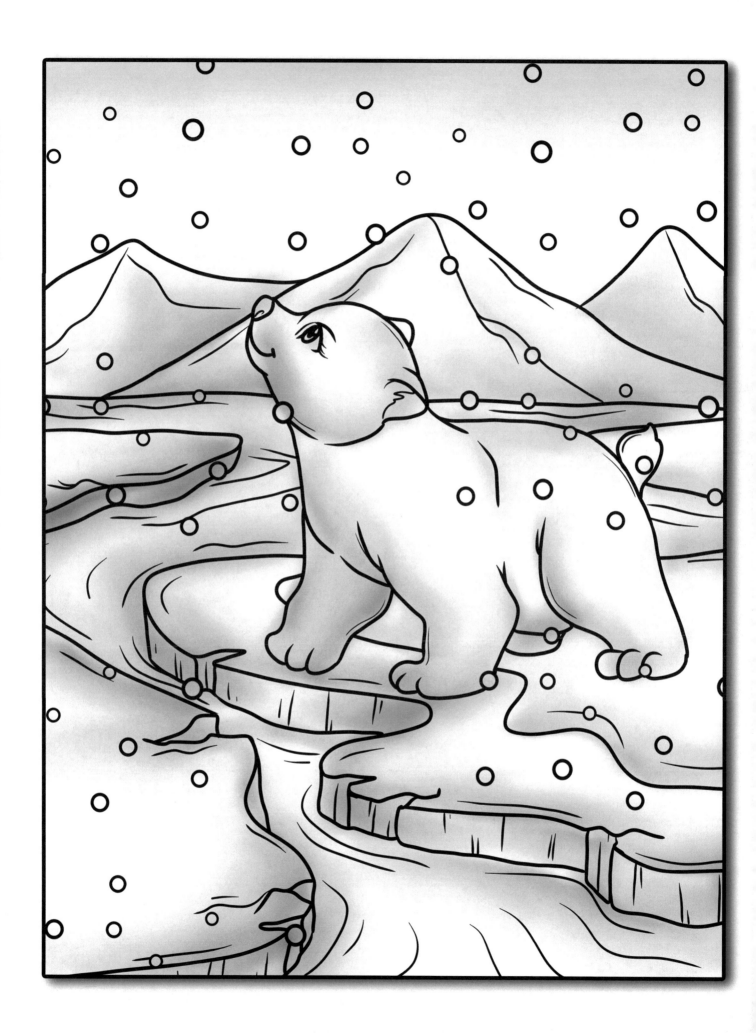

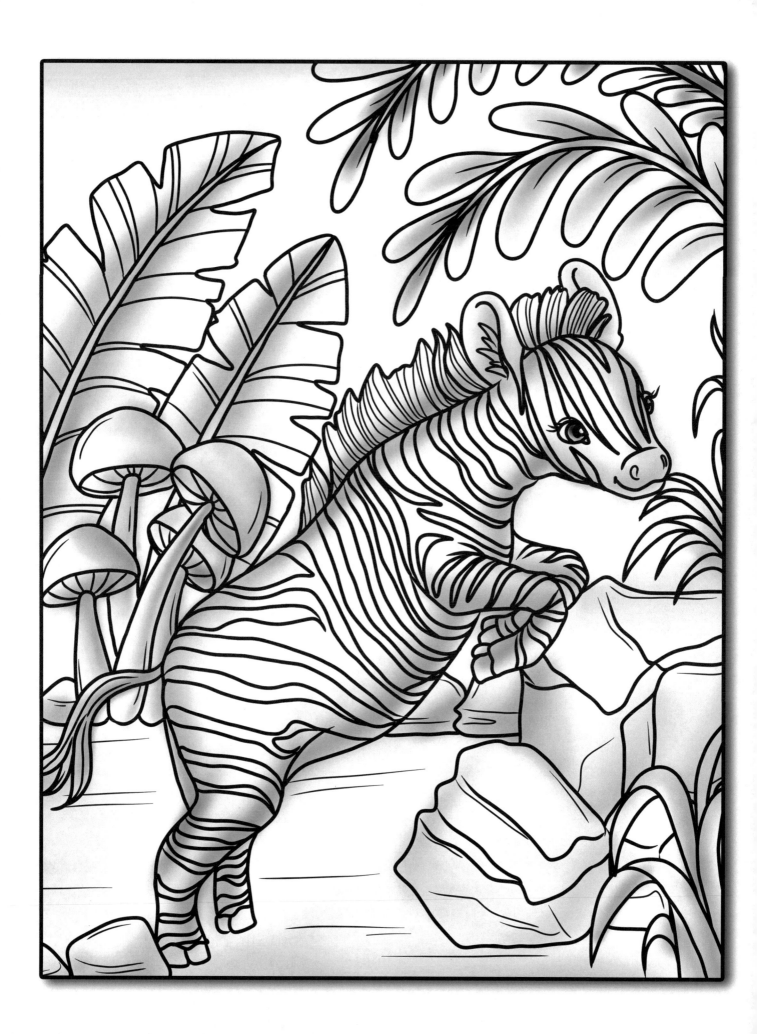

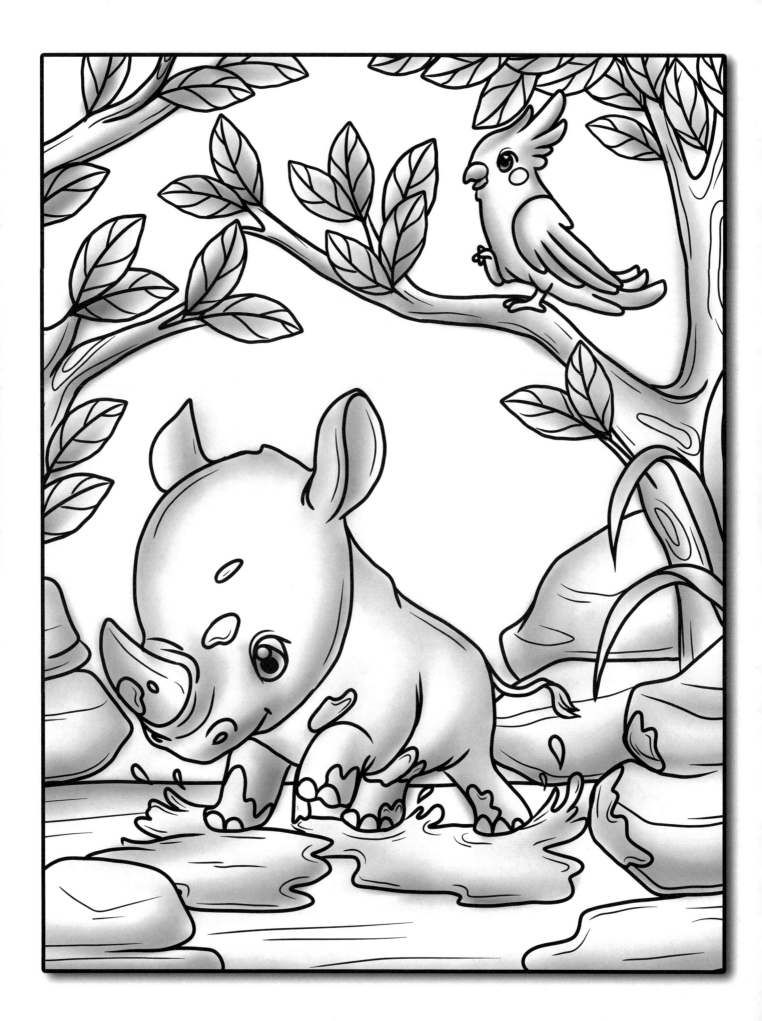

COLOR SWATCH TEST PAGE

COLOR SWATCH

BRAND: _____

PRODUCT NAME : _____

GET FREE COLORING PAGE

We publish a free coloring page regularly in our Facebook group. Join now, and let's have fun together!

FACEBOOK GROUP: DAMITA VICTORIA ARTWORK

LET'S BE FRIENDS

Damita Victoria

www.damitavictoria.com

DISCOVER OUR OTHER BOOKS THAT YOU'LL LOVE!

New-Fashioned Princesses	☐	Happy Season	☐
Adult Mandala Coloring Pages	☐	Calm and Cozy	☐
Beautiful Women	☐	Christmas Mandalas	☐
100 AMAZING Mandala	☐	Winter Aesthetic	☐
Fantastic Beauties Book One	☐	Lovely Garden	☐
Fantastic Beauties Two	☐	Whimsical Dreams	☐
Classy Princesa	☐	Flourish Swirls	☐
Relaxing Scenery	☐	Editorial Fashion	☐
Chill Out in Paris	☐	Positive Affirmations Book One	☐
Intricate Patterns	☐	Positive Affirmations Book Two	☐
Summer on the Farm	☐	Victorian Fashion	☐
Magical Wildland	☐	Love is Everwhere	☐
By The Beach	☐	Decorative Patterns	☐
Fantasticaland	☐	Zen Scenery	☐
Flowery Beauties	☐	100 Easy Flowers	☐
Happy Summer!	☐	Fantasialand	☐
Charmer Beauty	☐	Floating Life	☐
Freaky Night	☐	Magical Fairies	☐
Relaxing Winter	☐	Floral Mandalas	☐
Animal Reading Books	☐	Female Warriors	☐
The Witches	☐	Cozy Interiors	☐
100 Coloring	☐	Happy Easter	☐
Hello Autumn!	☐	Hello Spring!	☐
Mandala Flowers	☐	Amazing Patterns	☐
Fantastic Beauties Book Three	☐	Native American	☐
Beautiful Patterns	☐	Steampunk Art	☐
Relaxing Mandalas	☐	Birds and Nature	☐
100 Easy Mandalas	☐	Wolf Mandala	☐
Pin-Up Models	☐	100 Easy Coloring	☐

DISCOVER OUR OTHER BOOKS THAT YOU'LL LOVE!

100 Unique Patterns ☐

Mom's Daily Life ☐

Fairy Village ☐

Mermaids ☐

Summer Scenes ☐

Make Today Amazing ☐

Relaxing Patterns ☐

Global Beauties ☐

100 Easy Autumn ☐

Harajuku Fashion ☐

Chibi Princesses ☐

100 Mandalas ☐

Fantasy World ☐

Autumn Patterns ☐

Goddesses and Warriors ☐

Autumn Scenes ☐

50 Autumn Mandalas ☐

Victorian Chibi ☐

World of Animals ☐

Magical Unicorn ☐

Haunted House ☐

Vampires ☐

Freaks! ☐

100 Simple Flowers ☐

Winter Wonderland ☐

Jolly Winter ☐

100 Easy Winter ☐

Advent Calendar ☐

Shape and Beauty ☐

Christmas ☐

Dreamcatchers ☐

100 Lovely Swirls ☐

Mystical Patterns ☐

Angels ☐

Baby Animals ☐

WRITE AMAZON REVIEWS

WE'D LOVE YOUR FEEDBACK...

We'd love to know how everything worked out for you, don't be a stranger! Join the conversation and share your feedback with us.

Find this book on Amazon, scroll to the customer reviews, and please let us know your thoughts and comments.

We'd love to hear your feedback so we can continue to improve our service to you.